SEALS, SEA LIONS AND WALRUSES

SEA LIFE PARK/MONTE COSTA

SEALS, SEA LIONS AND WALRUSES

Dorothy Hinshaw Patent

HARCOURT BRACE & COMPANY
Orlando Atlanta Austin Boston San Francisco Chicago Dallas New York
Toronto London

This edition is published by special arrangement with
Holiday House, Inc.

Grateful acknowledgment is made to Holiday House, Inc. for
permission to reprint *Seals, Sea Lions and Walruses* by Dorothy
Hinshaw Patent. Text copyright © 1990 by Dorothy Hinshaw Patent.

Printed in the United States of America

ISBN 0-15-300361-8

5 6 7 8 9 10   059   04 03 02

Contents

SEALS, SEA LIONS AND WALRUSES

These California sea lions "fly" gracefully through the water.
JEFF FOOTT

1
Living in Two Worlds

UNDER THE CHOPPY SURFACE OF THE CLEAR BLUE WATER, THE dark forms flowed effortlessly, now heading up, then down, swirling in circles and twisting in figure 8s. They were seals, wonderfully designed to swoop and dive gracefully through the water, like giant birds flying through liquid air.

For more than 23 million years, seal-like animals have swum the seas of Earth, perfecting their skills with each generation. Whales and dolphins have become completely adapted to life in the water and never come ashore. But seals kept the ability to live on land at the same time they became increasingly at home in water.

The word "seal" can be used to refer to three families of mammals, all called "pinnipeds." The name is a reference to their unique finlike feet and means "wing- or fin-footed." One family, the Phocidae, includes what are called the "true seals," for they were the first to be described by science. The second family (Otariidae) consists of fur seals and sea lions, while the third (Odobenidae) is reserved for just one kind of animal, the walrus.

Similarities and Differences

Pinnipeds are big, ranging in size from the female ringed seal, which weighs about 85 pounds (38.6 kilograms), to the giant bull southern elephant seal, tipping the scales at 8,500 pounds, more than four tons (3.6 metric tons). They are relatively long-lived animals, with a life span of more than 20 years.

What makes a seal different from a sea lion? For one thing, sea lions and fur seals have a small external ear, while seals have only a small hole where the internal ear opens to the outside. For this reason, sea lions and fur seals are called "eared seals."

Pinniped limbs are highly modified for swimming. The bones of both the front and back legs are short and stout. The

Sea lions have a small external ear.
SEA LIFE PARK / MONTE COSTA

Seals, like this young northern elephant seal, have no external ear.
WILLIAM MUÑOZ

hind leg bones of all pinnipeds are buried inside the body so that the flippers begin at the ankle. The front flippers of true seals begin at the wrist, while those of the other pinnipeds start in the middle of the arm bone. Both fingers and toes are very long and are connected by the abundant webbing between them. The bottoms of eared seal flippers are naked, whereas those of true seals are furry.

Seals seem to have gone farther on the evolutionary path toward living in the water than sea lions and fur seals. In general, seals spend more time in the water and dive more deeply than do sea lions and fur seals. When seals move across rocks or beaches, they move mainly by waves of muscle contractions of their bodies, making them look a bit like giant, fat caterpillars. Some kinds also use the front flippers

You can see the long finger and toe bones in the harbor seal skeleton.
ALISA SCHULMAN

This northern elephant seal moves on land in typical seal fashion, dragging its hind flippers.
ALISA SCHULMAN

to lift the body as they move. The hind flippers just follow limply behind. Sea lions and fur seals, however, actually walk on land, even if it is a clumsy walk. They turn the hind flippers forward like short legs and waddle along. Sea lions can even run with a lopsided looking gait.

In water, true seals use the hind flippers to propel their bodies forward, while the forelimbs are used mainly for steering and balance. When a seal swims rapidly, the hind flippers stroke powerfully from side to side as the rear half of the body moves back and forth. The front flippers fit tightly into depressions along the sides of the body so that the animal moves smoothly through the water. Sea lions and fur seals, however, use the front flippers as oars in swimming, like penguins and sea turtles.

Walruses are easy to recognize because of their long tusks. The tusks are actually huge canine teeth. Both male and female walruses have tusks. Like true seals, the walrus has no external ear and uses its hind limbs to push itself through the water. But its flippers look more like those of fur seals and sea lions.

Sea lions, like this California one, use their hind flippers to help them walk.
MARC A. WEBBER

Walruses are easy to recognize because of their tusks and stiff whiskers.
KATHY FROST

WHERE DID SEALS COME FROM?

One big mystery about these animals is their evolutionary origin. Scientists can't agree whether all three families came from the same ancestor or whether they originated from two different ones. They are also not sure whether walruses are more closely related to sea lions or to true seals.

The earliest known pinniped is called *Enaliarctos*, which lived about 22.5 million years ago. While bits of skulls and teeth of this creature had been found before, it wasn't until 1989 that the complete skeleton was described, even though it was collected from rocks in central California in 1975. Scientists can learn a great deal about how an animal lived by studying its bones. The bones indicate more than the size and shape of the animal. One major function of the skeleton is to provide attachment points for the muscles. By noting how large the attachment points are, scientists can tell which muscles were biggest and thus, how the animal moved about.

The skeleton of *Enaliarctos* shows that primitive pinnipeds used all four limbs and also the muscles along their spines for swimming. Like sea lions and fur seals, *Enaliarctos* could turn its hind flippers forward for walking on land. As a matter of fact, its hindlimb bones have large attachment points for certain muscles, indicating that it probably was more active on land than the pinnipeds of today.

For many years, scientists agreed that fur seals, sea lions, and walruses all evolved from some early bearlike animal. They felt that true seals, on the other hand, came from a different ancestor that was more like an otter. Bears and otters belong to the same larger group, the doglike carnivores. But the skeleton of *Enaliarctos* shows some traits that are shared by all three pinniped families. Perhaps pinnipeds don't have two different ancestors after all.

Modern chemistry also provides evidence that the three groups of pinnipeds might have the same ancestors. Scientists studied three different proteins from pinnipeds and found that they were more similar to one another than they were to the proteins from doglike carnivores. Like these proteins, the DNA (the basic blueprint molecule of life) from different pinnipeds is more similar than it is to DNA from bears. This evidence indicates that all pinnipeds had the same ancestor. If this is true, then pinnipeds separated from their closest relatives about thirty million years ago, and the eared and true seals split from one another twenty to twenty-five million years ago. The evidence also points to walruses having evolved from eared seals about five million years after the separation from the true seals.

LIVING AT SEA

In addition to their webbed flippers and reduced outside ears, pinnipeds have other adaptations to a sea-going life. Swimming in the water provides a very different environment for animals than does walking on land and moving through the air. Water is much denser than air. Any parts that stick out from the body cause drag as the animal swims. The bodies of pinnipeds are streamlined in shape, tapered at both ends to glide through the water. Like penguins, whales and dolphins, they have no noticeable neck. Their heads blend smoothly into the outline of the body.

Like other pinnipeds, California sea lions have a streamlined shape, with no obvious neck.
CHIP MATHESON

The waters where most pinnipeds live are cold, and water can pull heat away from bodies as much as twenty-three times faster than air can. As mammals, pinnipeds maintain a high body temperature, so they must have ways of protecting themselves from heat loss. Their large size is one thing that helps keep their bodies warm in cold ocean waters. The larger and rounder a body is, the less surface area it has for its volume, so it's easier to keep a large, rounded body warm than a small, thin one.

The bodies of pinnipeds are also well insulated to hold in heat. They have a thick layer of fat called blubber under the skin, just as dolphins and whales do. The blubber helps protect the body from heat loss and also stores food energy.

Most mammals that live in cold places have a thick coat of fur to help keep them warm. Fur, however, can cause drag against the water when an animal swims. The pinnipeds that spend the most time swimming—the elephant seals—have very short hair. Only fur seals have a thick coat of fur that helps insulate them from the cold.

This young northern elephant seal has lots of blubber under its skin, and its fur is short.
BERND WÜRSIG

Living in two worlds can cause problems with keeping cool as well as with staying warm. Physical activity on land, such as fighting among males, can overheat the body. The sun can be warm even when the water is cold. For these reasons, pinnipeds often have to guard against overheating. The blood circulation of pinnipeds can be altered to help regulate body temperature. Special valves allow the blood supply to be diverted away from the skin and underlaying blubber when the animal is in the water to help keep in warmth. But when it is on land and needs to cool off, the circulation to these outer layers can be increased so that heat is lost as the blood circulates close to the body surface. This works well in true seals and walruses, which have short fur. When fur seals and sea lions get too warm, the circulation to the bare surfaces of their flippers increases. Eared seals sometimes wave their flippers in the air to aid in cooling off.

The senses of pinnipeds must also be able to work well in the sea as well as on land. While they have only a small outer ear or none at all, these animals have good hearing and use their voices to communicate loudly both in water and on land. Their large eyes allow them to see well in the dim light under the water's surface and they have stiff whiskers which are sensitive to touch.

DEEP DIVERS

Like other mammals, pinnipeds breathe air. In order to feed, they need to be able to survive for long periods without breathing. They also must have ways of avoiding the problems associated with the water pressure of the deep. Without mechanical aids, humans can barely dive to a depth of 30 feet (9.1 meters). But pinnipeds have great abilities to dive deeply and to stay down for long periods of time.

Pinnipeds have a variety of adaptations for diving. They

Elephant seals flip sand over their bodies on hot, sunny days to help cool off.
WILLIAM MUÑOZ

have greater blood volume than other mammals. Their blood contains more red blood cells with the hemoglobin that carries oxygen through the body. Their muscles contain a great deal of myoglobin, a protein similar to hemoglobin. The myoglobin makes the muscles look almost black in color. Like hemoglobin, myoglobin stores oxygen.

When pinnipeds dive, the blood circulates mostly to the brain, and body organs such as the liver and kidney reduce their oxygen use. Thus, they use less oxygen than when they are breathing. Their heart beat may also slow down to a tenth of the normal rate.

When humans dive deeply, nitrogen from the air in the lungs becomes dissolved in their blood. This happens because the pressure on the body increases with depth, and gases like nitrogen dissolve more readily in liquids like blood under pressure. If a human diver surfaces too quickly, the nitrogen becomes a gas again, forming dangerous bubbles in the blood. Seals don't have this problem. When they dive, their lungs collapse, and any air moves into the windpipe. Unlike the lungs, the windpipe doesn't have tiny blood vessels that allow gases to be absorbed into the blood. The nitrogen isn't taken into the blood where it can cause trouble.

The Weddell seal, which lives on the ice in south polar seas, is especially well adapted to diving. Weddell seals often dive deeply, from a thousand to 1,300 feet (300 to 400 meters). They can go as far down as 2,000 feet (600 meters). A Weddell seal has about two and a half times as much blood as a human of the same size. Its blood also contains a higher percent of hemoglobin. These two facts put together mean that its blood can carry about three times as much oxygen as the blood of a person. The muscles of a Weddell seal contain around ten times as much myoglobin as do human muscles, further increasing its oxygen carrying capability.

When a Weddell seal dives, it normally stays under no longer than 20 minutes. On such dives, the muscles work in the normal way, and oxygen is used with carbon dioxide as a waste product. The blood carries the carbon dioxide away. The seal can then dive again after a rest of only a few minutes. But if a dive lasts more than 30 minutes (a Weddell seal has been timed underwater for 73 minutes) the animal's metabolism changes. The muscles work in a less efficient way, but a way that doesn't use oxygen. Under these conditions, a waste product called lactic acid builds up in the muscles. The body can only tolerate a limited amount of lactic acid, and it takes oxygen to get rid of it. After a 45-minute dive, the seal

A Weddell seal heads into the water on a dive.
GERRY ELLIS/ELLIS WILDLIFE COLLECTION

must breathe for an hour to eliminate all the wastes in its body.

HUNTERS OF THE SEA

All pinnipeds are hunters, feeding on various kinds of sea birds, fish, squid, or shrimplike sea animals. Most are generalists, meaning that they eat whatever comes their way. If fish are bountiful, they will eat fish. But when there are plenty of squid, they will switch to squid. In the cold waters near the poles, small shrimplike animals called krill are very abundant. Many pinnipeds feed on krill. The crabeater seal, which lives in the Antarctic, specializes in eating this nutritious food. Its teeth have complicated bumps and ridges that form a sieve when held close together. The crabeater seal takes in a mouthful of krill and then forces the water out through the small gaps between the tooth ridges, keeping the krill in its mouth.

Another Antarctic species, the leopard seal, also feeds on krill. Another favorite prey of leopard seals is penguins. They also eat other birds, squid, fish, and seal pups. Leopard seals have especially large heads and wide mouths, making it easy for them to capture and eat large prey. They live along Antarctic shores, sometimes cruising near the rookeries of penguins looking for unwary victims. It takes only five minutes for a leopard seal to take the meat off a penguin's skeleton, biting off big chunks and leaving the bones, legs, flippers, and head.

Quite a few pinnipeds feed on the pups of other pinniped species. Walruses and sea lions are especially likely to do so. In Alaska, Steller sea lions are major enemies of northern fur seals, eating up to 6 percent of the pups every year on one island.

The leopard seal preys on animals both large and small.
MARC A. WEBBER

Having a Family

All pinnipeds go ashore to have their families. Small islands, which are likely to be free of land-living predators that might attack them, are favored breeding sites. Isolated beaches and offshore ice are also used. Large numbers of the same species usually gather in the same areas, called rookeries, for breeding. This makes it easier for males and females to find one another for mating.

Pinnipeds normally give birth to only one pup each year. Unlike puppies and kittens, most pinniped pups are born with their eyes ready to open. Their flippers are already strong and can flap about. Some, like harbor seals, can even swim right away.

The pups feed on the rich milk of their mothers and grow very fast. Seal milk is thick and oily, with plenty of nutritious

A California sea lion rookery.
BERND WÜRSIG

fat and protein. It has very little sugar and usually is less than half water. This makes it very different from the milk of mammals that live on land, which has a fair amount of sugar and is more than three-quarters water. Pinniped pups need rich milk both so they can build up their insulating blubber and so they can grow quickly.

Female pinnipeds come ashore only a few days before their pups are born. The birth process is usually quite fast, and the streamlined bodies of the young may be born either head first or tail first. After birth, the mother and pup sniff one another and make special identifying sounds. Each one learns the smell, voice, and/or appearance of the other so they can find each other in the often crowded rookery.

When female true seals have their young, they usually stay with them for only a short time. The mothers store up lots of fat before giving birth and eat little or nothing during the ten days to seven weeks that the pups are with them. Sea lions and fur seals, on the other hand, grow up more slowly. After a few days, the mothers leave their young to feed, returning

A Steller sea lion giving birth.
ROGER L. GENTRY

A New Zealand fur seal nurses her yearling pup.
ROGER L. GENTRY

to the rookery after being absent as long as a week. But instead of being weaned after a short time, eared seal off-spring stay with their female parent for four months to three years.

Male pinnipeds, called bulls, play no role in bringing up the young. They only come to the rookeries to mate. Males are often much larger than females, especially among the eared seals. In many species, males fight with one another for territories within the rookeries. Only full grown males with plenty of experience manage to win territories. They are called beachmasters. The strongest beachmaster gets the best territory, an area where lots of females will gather to give birth and raise their young. This beachmaster will have the best chance of mating with the most females, called cows.

Cows breed at a younger age than bulls. Breeding age varies among species, but females generally first mate when from two to four years old. Bulls are usually not ready to breed until they are at least six years old.

Steller sea lion bulls fighting for territory. The male on the left has been defeated and is giving a submission display (mouth open, chin up) prior to fleeing. Note the smaller, paler females around them.
ROGER L. GENTRY

In most species, females are ready to mate two or three weeks after giving birth. The embryo develops into a ball of cells called a blastocyst. In most mammals, the blastocyst becomes attached to the wall of the uterus as soon as it develops. This process is called implantation. After implantation, nourishment is brought to the developing embryo by the mother's bloodstream, and the young animal grows and develops. But in pinnipeds, the blastocyst floats around in the uterus without growing for two to five months. Then it implants and continues its development. This "delayed implantation" makes it possible for pinnipeds to breed while gathered together at the rookeries and still give birth almost a year later.

Pinnipeds generally return to the same area to breed each year, perhaps to the same spot where they were born. Northern fur seals, for example, breed on islands in the Bering Sea between Alaska and the Soviet Union. They migrate long distances to feeding areas as far away as Japan to the west and San Diego to the east. But when springtime comes, they return to the rookeries and give birth within ten yards of the same spot each year.

PINNIPED ENEMIES

Besides other pinnipeds, which may eat pups, the main natural enemies of these big animals are sharks and killer whales. Seals are often seen with scars that look like they were made by the teeth of big sharks like the great white. Killer whales live in packs called pods, and the animals in a pod may cooperate in hunting. Once while a scientist watched, several killer whales rushed toward an iceberg where a seal rested, making a big wave that toppled the iceberg and dumped the seal into the water. Killer whales will also chase seals right onto shore, letting the waves bring their huge bodies onto the beach where they can grab a seal. Polar bears prey on ringed seals in the Arctic. But as we'll see later, human beings are by far the worst enemies of pinnipeds.

This killer whale is attacking a sea lion on the beach.
JEFF FOOTT

2

Elephant Seals–the Ultimate Pinnipeds

Despite their variety, pinnipeds share a basic life style based on their unique dependence on both land and water. Males are generally larger than females. Breeding usually involves bulls competing with one another for mates, with dominant males mating with many cows. The animals return to the land to breed and feed at sea, and they are well adapted to diving to obtain food.

Elephant seals are the extremists among pinnipeds. They are the largest, they dive the most deeply, competition among males is the fiercest, and they are probably the most studied by scientists. Año Nuevo State Reserve, where hundreds of northern elephant seals haul out every year, is located only an hour away from the University of California at Santa Cruz. Researchers, first from Stanford University, then from the University of California, have studied the seals since 1962. By looking at what they have learned about these amazing animals, we can get an idea of how pinnipeds live and what makes them such successful survivors.

A young northern elephant seal takes a nap.
WILLIAM MUÑOZ

NEAR EXTINCTION

The northern elephant seal once bred from Point Reyes, north of San Francisco Bay, south to islands along the coast of Baja California in Mexico. Then the sealers came and slaughtered the seals for their abundant and useful oil. Seal oil had a variety of uses—as fuel for lamps in the days before electricity, as a lubricating oil, and as an ingredient in paint, clothing, and soap. One bull elephant seal could yield over

200 gallons of oil. Elephant seals are not afraid of humans, so they were easy marks for the hunters. By 1860, the sealers managed to reduce the population to so few animals that they were no longer considered worth hunting. By 1884, no more of these magnificent animals could be found, despite the efforts of museums to find specimens for their collections. The northern elephant seal was thought to be extinct.

Then, in 1892, a collector for the Smithsonian Institution found eight elephant seals on a remote island off Baja California; he promptly killed seven of them. Luckily, those eight were not all that remained, but scientists estimate that only between 20 and a hundred remained, all breeding on the same island.

In 1922, the Mexican government gave the seal colony legal protection, and the United States followed suit a few years later when the animals began to appear off the California coast. From that time, the population of northern elephant seals has increased at an incredible rate, repopulating the areas where it once lived, until today it has reclaimed most of its former range.

THE DRAMA OF THE ROOKERY

Every December, along the coasts of Mexico and California, an annual ritual takes place. One by one, northern elephant seal bulls lumber onto the beaches from the sea, ready to begin the rituals of conquest and mating. These huge animals look like prehistoric monsters, their enormous chests covered with protective sheaths of thick scarred skin, their noses enlarged into the flabby extensions that give them their name.

As the bulls arrive, they challenge one another, flinging their heads back and making unearthly noises that resonate through their inflated noses. The sounds have been described as similar to blowing across the top of a gigantic empty bottle,

The nose on this male northern elephant seal is so long that it hangs down into his mouth as he calls out his challenge.
FRANK S. BALTHIS

An older male northern elephant seal fights with a younger one, which has a much less developed nose.
WILLIAM MUÑOZ

to a car engine in need of a muffler, to weird thumpings inside a cave. When one bull challenges another, the second animal can retreat or answer back with its own strange sounds. If neither bull backs down they rush together, ramming one another and stabbing down at each other's chests with their long, sharp canine teeth. The fights are usually short, but can last as long as 45 minutes, leaving the bulls exhausted and bleeding.

For a month, the males are alone on the beach, fighting their battles and staking out their breeding territories. It takes nine years for an elephant seal bull to become big enough and sufficiently experienced to claim a choice stretch of beach. The competition is so strong that a beachmaster is unlikely to be successful for more than two or three years. An experienced elephant seal beachmaster can control a harem of about 50 cows. Where more than that number gather, several beachmasters may have adjoining territories, with younger and weaker bulls constantly patrolling around the edges of the harem, looking for a chance to mate while the beachmaster is otherwise occupied.

In January, the cows begin to arrive. The size difference between males and females is enormous in this species. Females are a third to a fourth the size of the gigantic, two-ton males. The females look like any other seal, showing no sign of the enlarged nose of the males. They come on shore only six days before their pups are born, and a male claims any and all females that land along his stretch of beach. Even after the females arrive and the pups are born, the males continue to challenge one another, and fights are common.

Mothers nurse their pups for four weeks. Each stays close to her pup, protecting it as best she can from the huge bulls that often thunder through the rookery during their battles and their retreats, crushing any pups in their path. The rookery is crowded and noisy, the bleats of youngsters separated

The female elephant seal is much smaller than the male and doesn't have an enlarged nose.
THOMAS JEFFERSON

A female northern elephant seal with her newborn pup.
FRANK S. BALTHIS

from their mothers mixing with the barks of the females and the hollow thumping sounds of the males.

After the pups are weaned, the females are ready to breed, although the males try to mate with them sooner. A successful beachmaster may breed with a hundred females in one season. As a cow finally heads for the water, leaving her fat pup behind to fend for itself, she is likely to encounter many bulls that were unsuccessful in battle, and they try to mate with her as well. But once she gets beyond the breakers, she is free until it is time to give birth again.

THE ANNUAL FAST

Like most true seals, adult elephant seals don't feed during the breeding season. The males go for three months without food or water, using the energy stored in their abundant blubber to fuel their constant battling. They lose about a third of their weight during this time, each burning hundreds of pounds of fat. When they arrive at the rookery, the males are glossy and plump. At the end of the season, after all the females have left, the exhausted, thin males may sleep for days before heading out to sea to regain the weight they have lost.

An exhausted northern elephant seal bull at the end of the breeding season.
PIETER AREND FOLKENS

Even more amazing than the fasting bulls, however, are the fasting cows. The cows do not feed for 34 days, a much shorter time than the bulls. But while the bulls burn calories fighting, chasing and mating, the fasting cows produce enough milk to quadruple their pups' weight in just four weeks. The pups grow from an average of 84 pounds (38 kilograms) at birth to 300 pounds (136 kilograms) when they stop nursing. That's a weight gain averaging about seven pounds (3 kilograms) each day! In the process, each female loses about 44 percent of her own body weight.

After the females leave their pups and mate, they return to the sea to feed and regain the weight they lost nursing their demanding pups. Meanwhile, the pups have stayed on shore. When the pups are weaned, about 50 percent of their weight is fat. They have plenty of stored energy to keep them going while they remain on land for eight to twelve weeks. During this time they molt from their dark birth coat to a lighter, silvery one. The pups, now called weaners, stay together in groups inland from the noisy, dangerous harems where they could be crushed by the heedless bulls. They play together, the young males already testing their fighting skills.

When they are six to seven weeks old, the weaners become interested in the water. At first they only visit the shore at sunrise and sunset, venturing just far enough to dampen their bellies. But bit by bit, they learn to swim. Their first efforts are very clumsy. But in only a week, they are accomplished swimmers and dip and dive together playfully. Their first dives are very short, but gradually they stay under longer and longer.

SUPREME DIVERS

Elephant seals are the champion divers among champs. Only in recent years have we been able to find out just how amazing these creatures are. The diving depths of other pinnipeds,

Weaners.
FRANK S. BALTHIS

especially Weddell seals and some species of fur seals, had been measured over a period of years. A device called a time-depth recorder, developed by Gerald Kooyman of Scripps Institution of Oceanography, was strapped onto the back of an animal which was then released. Weddell seals, which hunt under the Antarctic ice, always come back to the same breathing hole, so recovering the recorder from them was easy. Nursing female fur seals return from feeding at sea for a few days to care for their pups, so the instruments could also be easily recovered from them.

Elephant seals presented new difficulties, since they spend months at sea feeding. The problem was finally solved by Burney LeBoeuf and his coworkers from the University of

California at Santa Cruz by taking advantage of the habits of the females at the end of the breeding season. After feeding at sea for about 70 days, the females return to the then quiet beaches to molt, shedding their old coat of fur and the top layer of skin. The scientists used marine epoxy glue to attach the recorder to the females' fur and added small radio transmitters so the animals could be located when they came onshore again. When the signal indicated that a cow had landed, the scientists would speed to the beach in a rubber boat, sedate the seal, and remove the recorder.

The results of their study have been amazing. The first elephant seal equipped with a recorder dove farther than the previous record of 1,980 feet (600 meters). Over the years, three females dove more than 3,300 feet (1,000 meters), the limit of the recording device. LeBoeuf estimates that one of these dives was at least 4,125 feet (1,257 meters), more than four fifths of a mile into the ocean depths. The cow took only about 17 minutes to go down and another 17 to return to the

A male northern elephant seal at sea.
ALISA SCHULMAN

Female northern elephant seal wearing a time depth recorder.
THOMAS JEFFERSON

surface. And two minutes later, she headed down again, this time diving to 2,000 feet (610 meters) and followed that with dive after dive.

Unlike other pinnipeds studied with the time-depth recorder, elephant seals don't need to spend time resting at the surface between dives or between periods of diving. Female northern fur seals, for example, spend only about a quarter of their time diving while they are feeding at sea. The rest of the time they are resting or swimming near the surface. Weddell seals, which are such fine divers, can dive over and over again for a period of about 11 hours. They don't need long rests between dives unless the dives last more than 20 to 25 minutes. But after several hours of diving, Weddell seals spend from 11 to 13 hours on the ice resting. Some other pinnipeds can dive almost continuously for a period of three days. But elephant seals spend months out at sea, diving over and over again with little or no rest between dives.

Altogether, an elephant seal spends from 85 to 90 percent of its time at sea underwater. Even after an hour dive, the female elephant seal spends only about three minutes on the surface before heading again down for the depths. Elephant seals must somehow store enough oxygen in their bodies so that it doesn't run out, even on the longest dives.

Being able to spend so much time underwater means having plenty of time to hunt for food, so the female elephant seal quickly regains the weight she lost nursing her pup. She feeds on the abundant supply of fish and squid that spend the daytime deep in the sea and come closer to the surface at night. The female seal gains about two pounds (.9 kilograms) a day.

There is still much to learn about how elephant seals manage to dive so deeply and so often. How do they store so much oxygen? How do they avoid being harmed by the changes in pressure they encounter, which is as much as 125 times as great as it is at the surface? Scientists are hoping eventually to unravel the secrets of this amazing animal.

3

True Seals

ALTOGETHER THERE ARE 19 KINDS, OR SPECIES, OF TRUE SEALS. Most live in polar regions, feeding in the frigid water and hauling out onto the ice or rocks and islands offshore. For this reason, even people living along the coast rarely see them.

Seal pups generally don't enter the water for the first few weeks of life. They wait to learn to swim until they have been weaned, spending their early weeks staying in one place, growing and getting fat. Only harbor, Weddell, and Hawaiian monk seal pups have been seen going into the water with their mothers.

True seals are divided into two groups, northern seals and southern seals. The differences between the two are mainly in the skeleton, especially the skull. Northern seals also have larger claws on the hind flippers than do the southern seals. The front flippers of northern seals are short and stout, with strong claws. Southern seals have more variation in their front flippers. Some, such as monk seals, have short flippers with fairly large claws. But others, like the leopard seal, have long flippers with small claws.

Most northern seals, such as the bearded, ringed, harp, and spotted seals, breed on the ice. The gray seal can breed either on the ice or on land, while harbor seals use rocky

A Weddell seal rests on the ice. Its sharp claws help it move across the ice.
J. WARD TESTA

shores and beaches. Northern seals inhabit the northern seas. Among them, only harbor seals regularly live along the shores of the lower forty-eight states. The western Atlantic harbor seal sometimes strays as far south as the Carolina coast, and the Pacific harbor seal lives along the western coast of North America, all the way down to Baja California.

Southern seals show more variation, both in where they live and in their breeding habits. Elephant seals breed along coasts with mild climates, and the three species of monk seals live in tropical regions. But the other southern seals—the Weddell, Ross, leopard, and crabeater seals—are denizens of Antarctica and are superbly adapted to life on the ice.

Northern Seals

Harbor seals are found on both sides of the northern Pacific and northern Atlantic Oceans. They live along the shore, hauling out onto rocks and beaches. One seal may have its own favorite place where it always comes out of the water. There are two types of Atlantic harbor seal and two Pacific varieties.

The spotted seal is a close relative of the harbor seal that lives in northern Pacific seas. It is light gray in color, darker on top, and has abundant small dark spots.

The gray seal lives in both the western and eastern Atlantic. Adults are variable in color, with a brown, gray, or silver coat with dark spots. Pups are born with a white silky coat and molt to the adult pattern by the time they are four weeks old.

The ribbon seal is a striking animal with a black coat striped

Harbor seal mother and pup at Marine World Africa USA in Vallejo, CA.
D. BUSH/MARINE WORLD AFRICA USA

A spotted seal mother with her pup on the ice.
KATHY FROST

The male gray seal is somewhat larger than the female.
DR. JANET GODSELL

with white ribbons around the neck, base of the front flippers, and rear of the body. It is a solitary resident of the northern ice. Ribbon seals can move across the ice in a snake-like fashion as fast as a person can run.

The bearded seal is found all around the North Pole, staying as much as possible with the drifting ice floes, ever ready to head into the water for safety. Only in the summer do they haul out onto beaches. They are the largest of the northern seals. Adults reach seven feet (2.25 meters) in length and weigh about 550 pounds (250 kilograms). They have a thick set of long, stiff whiskers that give them their name.

The Baikal seal is the only completely freshwater seal. It lives in Lake Baikal in the southeastern part of the Soviet Union. Lake Baikal is the deepest lake in the world and has many interesting and unusual animals. Baikal seals are small,

Even the bearded seal pup has long whiskers.
KATHY FROST

A male ribbon seal on the ice.
KATHY FROST

reaching only about four feet (1.3 meters) in length, with a weight of 175 to 200 pounds (80 to 90 kilograms). They are dark gray, with a yellowish gray belly.

The Caspian seal is found only in the Caspian Sea, a landlocked salt water sea bordered by the Soviet Union and Iran. It is only slightly larger than the Baikal seal. The animals are dark gray, with grayish white undersides. Both males and females have spots. The male's spots are dark and tend to be all over the body. The female's are lighter and mostly on the back.

The hooded seal is a strange animal that lives in the North Atlantic and Arctic Oceans. The adult males have an enlargement of the nasal cavity that can be inflated, forming a black hood over the top of the head as big as two footballs. They also have a stretchy part of the tissue that separates the two halves of the nose. The tissue is bright red in color and can be ballooned out of either nostril, but usually the left one is used. The hood and balloon are often inflated when the animal is disturbed and also during mating season. But they may sometimes balloon up when the animal is at rest, so the function of the hood and balloon isn't completely understood.

THE HARP SEAL

Harp seals get their name from the horseshoe shaped marking on the sides and back of the body. In males, the head and "harp" are black, while the rest of the body is light silvery gray. The head and harp marking on the female are lighter in color, and the "harp" pattern may be broken up into spots. Males and females are the same size, about five feet (1.6 meters) long and weighing around 300 pounds (136 kilograms). Harp seals are well adapted for life on the ice. Their thick blubber protects the adults from the cold. They use their sharp strong claws on their front flippers to pull themselves out of the water and to move across the ice.

Female harp seal.
GERRY ELLIS/ELLIS WILDLIFE COLLECTION

Harp seals breed on offshore ice in mid- to late winter in three areas. One is around Newfoundland, the second in the Arctic Ocean northwest of Norway, and the third in the northwest corner of the Soviet Union, in the White Sea. The females come onto the ice a few days before giving birth and gather together in groups numbering tens of thousands. The females keep their distance from one another, however, snarling with noses pointed upwards.

The harp seal pup is born with a silky white coat. This thick fur layer keeps the pup warm while it builds up its protective blubber. It nurses for only 10 to 14 days. For the first two days, the mother never leaves her pup's side. After that, she is with it only about 15 percent of the time. The pup spends most of its time lying still, not wasting any precious

A harp seal pup nursing.
GERRY ELLIS/ELLIS WILDLIFE COLLECTION

energy moving around. The pups gain four to five pounds (about 2 kilograms) a day, while the mother loses two pounds (about 1 kilogram) for every one her pup gains. After weaning, the female leaves the ice to mate in the water with one of the males waiting there. She then takes off to feed in the sea and regain the weight she lost, leaving her pup behind.

The ice is beginning to melt and drift at the time of breeding, so it is important for the young to develop quickly. The newborn seal weighs 18 pounds (8 kilograms) at birth and increases to an amazing 77 pounds (35 kilograms) at weaning. The pups begin to lose their white fur when they are about 10 days old and by three weeks have grown a new gray coat with black spots. At this stage they are called "beaters." The pups normally don't enter the water and feed until they are a month old and have finished molting.

When the pups leave, they go one at a time. The adults, however, travel in large groups. After feeding for some weeks, they haul out on the ice again to molt, shedding their old coats and growing new ones.

THE RINGED SEAL—ARCTIC ANIMAL OF THE ICE

The ringed seal is a solitary species living on the ice around the North Pole, and as far south as Iceland and parts of Japan. The name comes from its unique coat, which has spots surrounded by white rings. Ringed seals are only about half the size of most other seals, weighing around 150 pounds (68 kilograms). They are about 4.5 feet (almost a meter-and-a-half) long.

Ringed seals spend most of the year living under the ice in fjords and bays. Each seal keeps a breathing hole open to the outside. The ice can be over six feet (two meters) thick, but the animal uses its sharp claws to keep the hole open. The ice over the hole is shaped like a cone, with only a small opening on top that lets in fresh air.

Often the seal will make a protected lair under the snow that builds up against ridges in the ice. The lair gives the animal a cozy protected place to rest, away from the wind.

Ringed seal females give birth inside a large lair. The pups are born with a soft, thick, white coat. They nurse for about two months, much longer than the harp seal. The ice used by ringed seals is called "fast ice," meaning that it is attached to the land. It is more stable than the moving ice used by harp seals, so it makes a longer lasting nursery.

Eskimo hunters and polar bears hunt ringed seals by finding their breathing holes or lairs. A hunter, either human or bear, may wait for hours beside a breathing hole waiting for the seal to surface and be caught. When trying to catch a seal

An Eskimo hunter with a ringed seal.
KARL W. KENYON

in its lair, the hunter sneaks up as quietly as possible, and crashes down on top of the lair, hoping to surprise the resting seal. Arctic foxes eat the seal pups, digging down into the lairs to get at their prey.

Before Eskimos came in touch with western culture, ringed seals were very important animals to them. The Eskimos ate the intestines and liver as well as the meat and blubber. The blubber also became oil for lamps and the furs were used for clothing and tents. The soft pup fur made well-insulated underwear, worn fur-side in.

SOUTHERN SEALS

While all northern seals except harbor seals live only in truly northern locations, the southern seals inhabit areas from Antarctica all the way to the Farallon Islands off San Francisco Bay, the northernmost breeding site of the northern elephant seal.

Southern elephant seals are much like their northern cousins, only bigger. These are the largest of all pinnipeds, with males as long as 16 feet (5 meters) long and weighing up to 6.6 tons (6 metric tons). The male southern elephant seal's inflatable nose is shorter than that of the northern species. The sound it makes is more of a rattling roar than the hollow, metallic sound of the northern elephant seal.

Four species of southern seals live only around Antarctica and the pack ice that surrounds the southern continent. The Weddell seal lives closest to the South Pole. It is a strange looking animal, with a long body and a small head. The Weddell seal is the only one that uses its teeth to keep its breathing hole open.

Not much is known about the solitary Ross seal. It is silvery gray in color, dark above and light below. Gray spots mark the line between the two colors along the sides, and

Weddell seals have small heads and large bodies.
ROGER L. GENTRY

Ross seal.
ROGER L. GENTRY

there are gray streaks on the throat. Ross seals eat mostly squid, but also fish and krill.

The krill-eating crabeater seal lives on the drifting pack ice in groups. Males and females are about the same size, 8.5 feet (2.6 meters) long. They are slim and have long noses.

The leopard seal has a wider range than the other Antarctic seals and regularly visits New Zealand. The females are bigger than the males and can reach 8.5 feet (2.6 meters). Adults are gray, darker on top, and have some spots along the sides, shoulders, and throat.

THE ENDANGERED MONK SEALS

Monk seals are unusual pinnipeds. They are the only kinds that spend their lives in warm waters. Even though their habitat is very different from that of other seals, these animals

The crabeater seal has teeth especially adapted for filtering krill.
J. WARD TESTA

don't have any obvious special adaptations for dealing with warmth. The Hawaiian monk seal does tend to rest in the shade or in damp sand during the day and hunt at night, which would help keep it from getting too hot. Like other seals, monk seals have short fur and a generous blood supply to the skin, which can aid in removing excess heat from the body.

Unfortunately, monk seals are especially sensitive to human interference. When the bond between the mother seal and her pup is disturbed, the pups can die from undernourishment. Scientists found in the 1950s that 39 percent of Hawaiian monk seal pups born during their study died before weaning, probably as a result of human disturbance.

Mediterranean monk seals inhabit sandy beaches, a popular place for people to relax. The pressure from humans has forced these seals away from the beaches. Now they are only found on small islands which people can't use because there is no fresh water, in sea caves with hidden underwater entrances, and on remote beaches along rocky shores. Fishermen view monk seals as competitors, too, so it is difficult for the seals to coexist where fishing activity is heavy, as in the Mediterranean.

The Mediterranean monk seal was familiar to the ancient Greeks, for its center of concentration was on Greek islands. Seals appear on their coins, and they harvested the animals for skins and oil. Perhaps 200 monk seals still live on Greek islands, with scattered populations also between Cyprus and Lebanon, along the Moroccan and Algerian coasts, and in the Black Sea. A few animals may survive along Yugoslavian and Tunisian shores, but the species is extinct on the mainland of Spain, France, Israel, and Egypt. Only a few hundred Mediterranean monk seals are left, and their numbers are falling.

The story of the Hawaiian monk seal is similar. This species lives in the Leeward Islands, a continuation of the Ha-

A female Hawaiian monk seal protects her pup.
KARL W. KENYON

waiian chain towards the northwest, and only a few hundred animals remain. World War II was especially hard on these animals, as some of the islands it inhabited were used for U.S. Navy bases.

The last sure sighting of the Caribbean monk seal was in 1952, although some may have been seen in the 1970s. Conservationists fear that this animal, first mentioned by Columbus in 1494, is extinct. An extensive search in 1979 found no seals and no evidence of their presence.

4

Sea Lions and Fur Seals

THE FOURTEEN SPECIES OF EARED SEALS, COMPRISED OF SEA
lions and fur seals, show less variation in appearance and life
style than do the true seals. Eared seals breed like elephant
seals, with males defending a harem of females. In all species,
the males are much bigger than the females. Northern fur
seals show the biggest difference, with bulls being up to five
times the size of the cows.

Male eared seals are generally darker in color than their
mates. Males tend to be blackish or brownish in color, while
females are more likely to be silver gray or golden brown.
Males of most species have longer, coarser hair over their
shoulders and chests. This hair probably helps protect them
from one another's bites during battle.

No eared seals are as specialized as the crabeater seal, although the Antarctic fur seal does feed mainly on krill. Eared
seals tend to live in areas where rising currents from the ocean
depths bring nutrients to the surface. In such places, sea life
flourishes, and there is usually plenty of food. Eared seals
may also catch animals that live on the sea floor, such as
octopuses and rock lobsters. But they do not dive as deeply as

The elephant seals on the right are much larger than the California sea lions on the left.
ALISA SCHULMAN

true seals. Eared seals may also eat penguins and pinniped pups.

Most eared seals live in cool rather than very cold waters. Three kinds, however—the Northern fur seal, the Steller sea lion, and the Antarctic fur seal—do live in water close to the freezing point. But no eared seals breed on the ice, and none has adapted to living in fresh water.

Eared seals spend more time on land than do most true seals. The front flippers of eared seals angle downward and out toward the sides instead of sticking out from the sides like those of true seals. The eared seal can support its body with its front flippers bent at the joints, its chest held up off the ground. Fur seal bulls gallop across the beach fast enough to catch up with a running person.

Mothers and Pups

While female true seals may fast for several weeks, a mother eared seal rarely fasts for more than a day or two at a time. She may leave her pup to feed for as long as seven days, so the pups must be able to fast that long without losing strength. When the mother eared seal returns to the rookery, she bleats for her pup. When the pup hears, it answers. Sometimes it takes awhile for the two to find each other on the crowded beach, but they are so good at recognizing one another's voices through the din of barking that they rarely fail to be reunited.

Eared seals that live in cool waters wean their young when they are four months old or older. Many wean the pup the

This female northern fur seal has returned to the rookery after spending about a week at sea feeding. She can recognize her own pup and won't allow any others to nurse.
KARL W. KENYON

following year, when a new pup is born. But those living in the harsher climates stay together even longer. The Galapagos fur seal pup, for example, remains with its mother until it is two or even three years old. A new pup is usually not born until the older one is weaned. In some species, such as Steller sea lions, a new pup is nursed along with a yearling and sometimes even a two-year-old.

KINDS OF SEA LIONS

The Steller sea lion is a common species that lives across the northern Pacific Ocean, from just south of Los Angeles on the east, northward across the Alaskan and Siberian coasts, and southward to the islands of Japan. This is the largest sea

A scarred Steller sea lion beachmaster is being challenged by another bull in the water, to the righ
KARL W. KENYON

The differences in size and appearance among bulls (the huge head), cows, and pups (the small, dark animal in front) is clear in southern sea lions.
JOHN FRANCIS

lion, with males reaching 10 feet (3 meters) in length and 1.1 tons (one metric ton) in weight. The females are about seven feet (2.2 meters) long and weigh 455 pounds (207 kilograms). Males have a thick, strong neck covered with a mane of coarse hair longer than the body hair. Adults are a yellowish tan color.

The southern sea lion lives along the South American coast, from Peru to Tierra del Fuego and up the eastern coast to Uruguay. The larger males are dark brown with a slightly lighter mane.

The Australian sea lion lives only along the coasts of Western and South Australia. The chunky males are chocolate brown and have a mane. The females are silvery gray to tan with creamy white bellies.

Hooker's sea lion, also called the New Zealand sea lion, lives only along the small islands of southern New Zealand,

Australian sea lion mother and pup.
GERRY ELLIS/ELLIS WILDLIFE COLLECTION

with a few reaching the southern tip of the South Island. These animals have shorter muzzles and more rounded faces than Australian sea lions. Males are black and have manes. The females look very much like those of the Australian sea lion.

The Familiar California Sea Lion

Probably the most familiar pinniped of all is the California sea lion, for this is the performing "seal" of circus fame and is found in most zoos. The California sea lion lives from British Columbia southward all along the coast of the western United States to Mexico at about the level of Tres Marias Island, south of the tip of Baja California. Populations are also found in the Galapagos Islands, with a few in Japan.

The California sea lion is chocolate brown in color. Males reach 7.8 feet (2.4 meters) in length and weigh around 660 pounds (300 kilograms), while females are six feet (1.8 meters)

Female (on the left) and male California sea lions.
SEA LIFE PARK/MONTE COSTA

California sea lion rookery.
JOHN FRANCIS

long and weigh about 220 pounds (100 kilograms). Males lack the mane of other sea lions, but they are chunkier than the females and have an obvious bump on the forehead caused by a crest of bone along the skull.

In southern California, California sea lions breed in the early summer. Males start fighting for territories about the same time the first pups are born. After the territories are established, fighting lessens, and males maintain their status with threats rather than battles. They bark, stare at one another, shake their heads, and lunge in threat.

The females gather together in harems and pay little attention to the males until they are ready to mate a couple of weeks after having their pups. Most females give birth in June. For the first three days or so, the mother stays with her pup constantly. If she needs to cool off in the water, she makes the pup come with her, pulling it along with her teeth if necessary. But soon, she is willing to leave it. As time goes on, mother and pup are separated for longer and longer periods. When the pup reaches three weeks of age, it only nurses for about a half hour each day. Since it stays with its mother and nurses until the next pup is born or even longer, the young sea lion doesn't need to grow and put on blubber rapidly like true seal pups must.

As the pups grow, they spend most of their time in groups resting and playing together. The rookery is a noisy place, with the bulls barking constantly and mothers and pups calling to one another.

California sea lions eat mostly octopus and squid but will also feed on fish when available.

California sea lions are intelligent and playful animals that learn easily, which explains their popularity as performers.

California sea lion with her pup at Marine World Africa USA in Vallejo, CA.
D. BUSH/MARINE WORLD AFRICA USA

California sea lion performing at Sea Life Park.
SEA LIFE PARK

They are talented acrobats, able to balance a glass of water on the nose while swimming over hurdles and climbing out of the water. A trained sea lion can balance a ball on its nose while climbing a ladder.

These animals can also be trained to understand commands in simple man-made languages in which arm signals given by researchers represent words. The sea lions that have learned these languages can respond correctly to a completely unfamiliar command, such as "Fetch the small ball and bring it to the Frisbee" the first time the command is given.

Fur Seals

Fur seals differ from sea lions in several ways. Sea lions in general are larger than fur seals. While sea lions have rounded snouts, fur seals have pointed ones. The Juan Fernandez fur seal and the Guadalupe fur seal have especially long pointed noses, which make them distinct even from other fur seal species. The flippers of fur seals tend to be longer than those of sea lions.

The biggest difference, however, is in the thick, soft coat which gives fur seals their names. The pinniped coat consists of stiff guard hairs and soft, wavy underfur. One guard hair and a cluster of underfur hairs grow together out of a single canal through the skin. Walruses have no underfur, and elephant and monk seals have only one to three underfur hairs for each guard hair. The northern fur seal, however, has 17 underfur hairs for every guard hair. When these animals shed, all the old underfur isn't molted, increasing the density of the coat to as many as 68 per guard hair in full grown males. Air is trapped in the underfur even when the fur seal swims, keeping the skin warm and dry.

Seven kinds of closely related fur seals live in southern waters. An eighth relative, the Guadalupe fur seal, breeds today only on Guadalupe Island off the coast of Baja Cali-

This northern fur seal shows the typical fur seal pointed snout.
ALISA SCHULMAN

Guadalupe fur seal.
C. ALLAN MORGAN

fornia. The Galapagos fur seal, which is found only on the shores of the Galapagos Islands, is the smallest. Males reach only around five feet (1.5 meters), and females are only a little bit smaller. Cape fur seals live along the coasts of Namibia and South Africa. They are the largest fur seal, with males about 7.5 feet (2.3 meters) long and weighing from 440 to 770 pounds (200 to 350 kilograms). The females are smaller and weigh about 260 pounds (120 kilograms).

The other six species live on offshore islands or along the coasts of South America, Australia, New Zealand, and Antarctica.

The Northern Fur Seal

Just one fur seal species lives in the far north. The northern fur seal is very abundant in the north Pacific and breeds on islands between Alaska and the Soviet Union. During the winter, it migrates southward about as far as San Diego to the east and just south of Tokyo to the west. In recent years, a population has begun to breed far south, on San Miguel Island off the California coast. Some of the animals discovered there were tagged as pups far to the north on the Pribilof Islands in the Bering Sea.

Adult male northern fur seals measure about seven feet (2.13 meters) and weigh between 400 and 600 pounds (182 to 272 kilograms). Females weigh only 95 to 110 pounds (43 to 50 kilograms) and are just five feet (1.5 meters) long. Bulls are dark brown, with some white hairs in their bushy manes. Females are gray, darker above and paler below. Males and females alike have a light blotch on the chest.

Northern fur seals breed in typical fur seal fashion. Males arrive at the rookeries early in June and battle to stake out territories. While males can breed as young as five years old, they aren't big, strong, and experienced enough to become beachmasters until they are about twelve. Each successful

Cape fur seal rookery.
ROGER L. GENTRY

Northern fur seal bull with his harem.
GERRY ELLIS/ELLIS WILDLIFE COLLECTION

This female northern fur seal is calling to her pup after feeding at sea.
JOHN FRANCIS

beachmaster controls about 50 cows. Cows begin to arrive around the middle of June and give birth only a couple of days later. They nurse their pups regularly for about a week, then mate. After mating, the females begin to feed again, spending six days at sea for every day the young nurse.

When the female comes ashore, she lands near where she left her pup and calls to it. Many hungry pups may answer her call. She sniffs them and threatens those that are not her own. While the mothers are particular, the pups are not. They will feed from any willing female.

While the mothers are away, the pups gather together in pods to play and sleep. They usually don't try swimming until they are around a month old. Pups are nursed for three months. Then they are on their own.

5

Walruses

THE WALRUS IS A STRANGE LOOKING ANIMAL, WITH ITS TWO
long tusks, square whiskered face, and heavy body. Walruses
share characteristics with both eared and true seals as well as
having unique traits all their own. Their flippers are more
like those of eared seals, with front flippers starting at the
middle of the forearm and hind flippers that can be turned
forward for moving on land. But walruses swim more like
true seals, with side-to-side movements of the hind flippers.
Like true seals, walruses have no external ear.

THE WALRUS AT HOME

There is only one species of walrus alive today. It lives in the
cold seas around the North Pole, along the coast of the Soviet
Union, around Greenland and Baffin Island, in Hudson Bay,
and also between Alaska and the Soviet Union.

Next to elephant seals, walruses are the second largest pinnipeds, with bulls reaching 10.5 feet (3.2 meters) in length
and 2,673 pounds (1215 kilograms) in weight. Females are
smaller, about 8.5 feet (2.6 meters) long and 1782 pounds
(810 kilograms). The top canine teeth of walruses grow into
long tusks. Males and females look similar, but the tusks of
females are slimmer, shorter, and more curved than those of

males. Adult males also have thickened skin on the neck and shoulders which has raised scarlike bumps lacking in females.

Walruses are creatures of the ice. Their odd appearance actually shows their special adaptations to their way of life. The huge tusks continue to grow throughout the animal's life. Those of males can reach three feet (about one meter) in length. The tusks serve a variety of functions. They are used to anchor the walrus as it climbs out of the water onto the ice, and to chop breathing holes. The scientific name of the walrus, *Odobenus*, means "tooth walker." The tusks are also used in threat displays. Generally, the males with the largest tusks are dominant and are able to mate with more females.

Adult walruses have a unique set of air sacs that grow from their throats. The walls of these pouches are elastic so that they can be inflated with air from the lungs. Walruses can sleep at sea, inflating their air sacs to keep their heads afloat so they can breathe.

Walruses gather together in large groups to rest. You can see the tusks, thick skin, and whiskers easily.
BERND WÜRSIG

Walruses are basically cinnamon brown in color. But old males are very pale, and young animals are darker. The bulls molt in the summer and lose all their hair for about a month during June and July. At this time, the pinniped adaptation of the circulatory system to living in cold water and then coming out into the sunshine becomes visible. A bull looks ghostly pale when it leaves the water because the blood vessels to the skin are shut down. But after it has lain in the sun for awhile, its skin becomes brick red as the circulation is again open and the animal needs to lose some body heat in the warmth of the sun.

The bull at the top of the photo has just come out of the water and is much paler than the other walruses.
JEFF FOOTT

You can see the worn-down whiskers and the thick skin of these walruses. Note that the tusks vary in length and that some have broken or worn tips.
KARL W. KENYON

How Walruses Feed

Walruses are unique among pinnipeds in their way of feeding. Instead of chasing after squid and fish, walruses glide slowly over the dark sea floor, their tusks brushing against the bottom and their abundant, sensitive whiskers feeling for clams and worms. Walrus skin over most of the body is very thick, probably protecting the animal from being punctured by the tusks of other walruses as they climb over one another and lie together on the beach. But the skin on the front of the snout is thin and sensitive. The whiskers of wild walruses are worn down, while those of captive animals become long, indicating that the whiskers are worn down during bottom feeding.

Walruses appear to be able to suck clams right out of their shells, for only the soft clam bodies are found in the walrus's stomach. Their sucking power is impressive. In captivity, walruses can suck a five-pound (2.3 kilogram) plug in the bottom of a water-filled pool out of its hole. Scientists have measured the suction of the walrus mouth, and it is definitely enough to suck out the soft parts of clams. The suction power is probably produced by the tongue acting along with the high-domed mouth cavity.

Walruses can also squirt water under high pressure, as zoo keepers have found out the hard way. No one has actually watched walruses feed. But we can imagine that they probably use the thick ridges of tough skin at the upper edge of the snout to help dig out clams and strong jets of water to excavate clam burrows. Killing a walrus with a full stomach of clams is a treat for Eskimos, for they wash the shelled clams and eat them. There can be as much as 108 pounds (49 kilograms) of cleaned clams in a walrus stomach.

WALRUS FAMILY LIFE

Female walruses are ready for mating during the winter. They gather together in small groups on the ice, while males display themselves in the surrounding water. In addition to displaying their tusks, the bulls make a variety of sounds, inflating their throat sacs to make bell-like underwater calls. Above the water, they bark, growl and whistle.

Females give birth in late spring, 15 months after mating. The newborn calf weighs 130 to 140 pounds (60 to 65 kilograms) and is about 3.6 feet (1.1 meters) long. It has short, soft fur and a white mustache. For the first six months, the

A female walrus with her calf.
LLOYD LOWRY

calf feeds only on its mother's milk. Bit by bit, it learns to feed itself. It stays with the mother for two years, when she has a new calf.

The newly independent young walruses join up with others of their own sex. Their tusks are still small, only about four inches (10 centimeters) long. Females are usually ready to breed when they are six to seven years old. Because of the intense competition for females, males are generally not successful at mating before they reach the age of 15.

Throughout their lives, walruses are social animals, traveling in groups and hauling out together onto ice and beaches. They seek the warmth of one another's bodies and lie piled together so thickly that no sand or ice is visible between their bodies.

Hunting Walruses

Walruses have always been an especially important animal to the Eskimos. The tusk ivory was once used to make smooth, durable sled runners. The hides, split in half, are still used to cover boats called oomiaks, while the intestines can become rain parkas. The air sacs become drums and food containers. The stomach contents, intestines, heart, flippers and meat provide food for both humans and dogs.

Walruses were hunted during the eighteenth through early twentieth centuries by European and North American hunters, like so many other pinnipeds, reducing their populations severely. But today, only natives are allowed to kill them, and only to meet their own needs. Walrus hides and meat still have their place in Eskimo life, but the tusks are more important economically, since carvings from walrus ivory have become very popular tourist items.

Native peoples have hunted pinnipeds and used their skins to make important products, like this skin boat. Their hunting is not a threat to pinniped survival.
KATHY FROST

6

Seals, Humans, and the Future

HUMANS ARE BY FAR THE WORST ENEMIES OF PINNIPEDS. DUR-
ing the eighteenth and nineteenth centuries, seal hunters
came very close to eliminating several species from the earth.
Seals have been prey for humans since the Stone Age. But
fast sailing ships, and later steamships, led to the slaughter of
millions of pinnipeds. The animals were clubbed at their
rookeries and netted at sea. Seal oil was used for lamps, and
seal skins for leather and fur.

The first victims were hooded and harp seals, along with
walruses, which gave ivory in addition to skins and oil. Fur
seals also became victims, and within only a few years, populations of hundreds of thousands of fur seals were almost
wiped out.

Amazingly enough, all the slaughter didn't result in extinc-
tions. When there were only a few animals left, it was no
longer economical to launch voyages to harvest them. Since
the late 1800s, many pinniped populations have been build-
ing back up, and most species are now in good condition.
Fortunately, these hardy animals have proven to be very re-

silient. Their lives and breeding behavior, with many pups killed by the huge bulls, may seem very strange to us. But clearly, pinnipeds are born survivors, very successful at living in the sea and breeding on land.

EXPLOITING FUR SEALS

The luxurious coat of fur seals helps keep them warm, and humans have valued the fur for both its warmth and its softness. The Guadalupe fur seal was brought almost to extinction by hunters during the eighteenth and nineteenth centuries. None were found by a scientific expedition in 1950. But in 1954, a few animals were found in a sea cave. Since then, the population has been growing. The Galapagos fur seal was also decimated by sealers, but didn't reach quite the lows of the Guadalupe species. The Juan Fernandez fur seal is found only on islands off the coast of Chile. Before seal hunting, this species was very common in waters around those islands. But, as with other kinds, hunters killed off most of the animals. Once believed to be extinct, they were rediscovered in 1965. Today, there are probably fewer than a thousand.

The stories go on and on. But perhaps the saga of the Antarctic fur seal is the most remarkable of all. Captain Cook discovered this species at South Georgia in Antarctica in 1775. The sealers who were working at the Falkland Islands off the tip of South America were quick to move southward. During 1800 to 1801, 17 ships from Britain and the United States harvested 112,000 Antarctic fur seal skins from South Georgia.

When the South Georgia population became almost extinct in 1822, sealers moved west to kill off the seals living on the South Shetland Islands. That took only three years. And so

The Juan Fernandez fur seal was once common. Fewer than a thousand are now left.
JOHN FRANCIS

Antarctic fur seal bulls.
C. ALLAN MORGAN

it went. Every time a new rookery of Antarctic fur seals was found, sealers came in and slaughtered the animals. Adult females and young males were the preferred victims, since they provided the best furs. By killing the females of breeding age, the sealers eliminated the chances for the species to recover its numbers.

No one knows for sure how many Antarctic fur seals survived in remote places. But fortunately, a few did, probably less than a hundred. Since then, this species has made an amazing recovery. Nowadays there are about a million Antarctic fur seals. One reason for the explosion of their population is probably the decline in whales that feed on krill in the Antarctic. With many fewer whales, the supply of krill is greater than ever before, and the fur seals have plenty to eat. Now there are so many seals that they are destroying the habitat used for breeding by a variety of bird species. What the future holds in store for the animals that depend on Antarctica for breeding is unknown.

THE HARP SEAL SLAUGHTER

Because they gather in such large breeding groups, harp seals have been easy prey for hunters. Both blubber and the pelts of young seals are taken. The soft white fur of the pups and the thick coat of the beaters are valuable.

Heavy hunting during the eighteenth and nineteenth centuries led to a drastic drop in harp seal numbers. As recently as 1951, Canadian scientists estimated that 645,000 pups were born, while 456,000 seals were killed. Considering that many young animals die before reaching adulthood, the number of animals harvested was too high.

Hunting of all three populations of harp seals is now controlled by the governments of the Soviet Union, Norway,

A harp seal touches noses with her new pup.
GERRY ELLIS/ELLIS WILDLIFE COLLECTION

Denmark (on behalf of Greenland), and Canada. Limits are set on hunting dates and on the number of seals harvested. Since the regulation of hunting, all three harp seal stocks have recovered. By the mid-1980s, there were about two-and-a-half million harp seals, making it the most numerous pinniped living in the North Atlantic Ocean. Today, this beautiful seal is in no danger of being over-harvested.

Harp seal hunting methods seem cruel, but the animals probably suffer no more than cattle at the slaughterhouse. But the image of men clubbing helpless young animals while their mothers watch is very upsetting. The hunters come on shore with clubs and strike the seals over the head, crushing their skulls. The dead or unconscious seal is then flipped over on its back, and the skin is cut down the midline of the belly. The blood vessels to the flippers are severed, and the animal is bled. The pelt is then removed from the body. The meat is mostly wasted.

Animal protection groups in the United States and Canada have fought to eliminate the hunting of the white-coated pups in Canada. They feel that the killing is inhumane. Seal pup fur has not been used for any essential purposes, just for attractive extras like fur coats. In 1983, the European Economic Community, which includes major western European countries, banned the importing of products made from baby seals. Since Europe was the main market, the hunters had nowhere to sell their furs. But it was still possible that new markets might be found. Fortunately, the hunt for baby harp and hooded seals ended officially in Canada at the end of 1987, when the government decided not to permit any more hunting of baby seals.

MODERN PROBLEMS

In 1972, the United States Congress passed the Marine Mammal Protection Act, which was renewed in 1988. This important law placed the control of marine mammals in the hands of the federal government instead of those of the states bordering on the oceans. It forbade the taking or importation of marine mammals or products made from them except under special, limited conditions. Native peoples are still allowed under this law to harvest whales, seals, and walruses to meet their own needs.

Until 1984, however, northern fur seals in the Pribilof Islands were regulated under a special treaty among Japan, Canada, Russia, and the United States that was signed in 1911. Hunting was allowed, but only young males were taken so that the breeding population would not be depleted. The herds increased to about two million in 1950. In 1956, the

Under the Marine Mammal Protection Act, natives like these Eskimos drying bearded seal skins are allowed to harvest pinnipeds for their own use.
KARL W. KENYON

population mysteriously began to decline, and the birth rate fell to only 40 percent of what it was in the early 1950s. In 1988, the Pribilof herd was given a new designation of "depleted" under the Marine Mammal Protection Act. Now these animals cannot be taken except for scientific purposes and to meet native needs.

Unfortunately, no one understands the slide in northern fur seal numbers. A variety of causes have been suggested. Perhaps too many seals were killed. From 1956 to 1968, 320,849 young female seals were killed because managers thought too many females were present, lowering the total rate of pregnancy. Pregnancy didn't increase, but the population continued to fall even after the killing stopped. So other factors were also involved.

Perhaps the fur seal's food supply decreased so it couldn't support as many animals. Commercial fishing for bottom fish,

No one understands just why northern fur seal rookeries like this one are producing fewer pups than in the past.
JOHN FRANCIS

the sorts fur seals eat, expanded greatly in the 1960s. But pups leaving the rookeries showed no decrease in weight from 1957 (the first year they were weighed) onward. Competition for food with humans may be part of the cause, but it's not the whole reason.

THE FUTURE OF PINNIPEDS

The decline in northern fur seals most likely has a variety of causes, most of them having to do with changes in the world brought on by humans. We have dumped pollutants into the seas. DDT and PCBs collect in the seals' bodies. Such contaminants have been blamed for the reproductive failure of harbor seals in Washington state and harbor seals in California. Ringed seals face a similar threat. PCBs appear to be harming reproduction of ringed seals in the Baltic Sea. While 80 to 90 percent of adult females become pregnant each year in the Canadian Arctic, where they are exposed to lower concentrations of PCBs, fewer than 25 percent of Baltic cows get pregnant. Biologists are worried that the heavy contamination of the Baltic with PCBs may lead to the end of ringed seals there.

Other problems make trouble for seals. A mysterious disease killed at least half the harbor seals off the Northern European coast in 1988. Scientists fear that the animals may have become susceptible to sickness because of the heavy pollution they have been exposed to from western European industry.

Fishermen pose dangers for seals, too. They sometimes blame pinnipeds for decreased catches, thinking the seals are eating too many fish. Even when it is illegal, fishermen who think their livelihood is in danger may kill seals. In recent years, huge plastic "drift nets" have become a popular fishing technique. Drift nets stretch for mile after mile and can entangle pinnipeds and other air breathing sea dwellers like dolphins and sea turtles, suffocating them. When the nets tear apart, pieces can float for years, killing unsuspecting animals as they move with the ocean currents. Fish nets and other plastic materials can also get stuck around the necks of seals, choking them or cutting into their skin as the animals grow.

How well other living things survive on our planet depends today on how we plan the uses of the land and how we deal with problems like chemical pollution and garbage. Now that so many pinniped species have come back from the brink of extinction caused by hunting, it would be tragic if they disappeared because of other kinds of human thoughtlessness.

This northern elephant seal became entangled in a rope, which is now becoming imbedded in its skin.
C. ALLAN MORGAN

Let's hope that animals like this graceful southern sea lion won't be forced into extinction by human greed, selfishness and insensitivity.
BERND WÜRSIG

Scientific and Common Names of Seals and Sea Lions

Family PHOCIDAE: True Seals

Northern phocids

Gray or Atlantic seal	*Halichoerus grypus*
Harbor or common seal	*Phoca vitulina*
Larga or spotted seal	*Phoca largha*
Ringed seal	*Phoca hispida*
Caspian seal	*Phoca caspica*
Baikal seal	*Phoca sibirica*
Harp or Greenland seal	*Phoca groenlandica*
Ribbon or banded seal	*Phoca fasciata*
Hooded or crested seal	*Cystophora cristata*
Bearded seal	*Erignathus barbatus*

Southern phocids

Mediterranean monk seal	*Monachus monachus*
Caribbean monk seal	*Monachus tropicalis*
Hawaiian or Laysan monk seal	*Monachus schauinslandi*
Weddell seal	*Leptonychotes weddelli*
Ross seal	*Ommatophoca rossi*
Crabeater seal	*Lobodon carcinophagus*
Leopard seal	*Hydrurga leptonyx*
Southern elephant seal	*Mirounga leonina*
Northern elephant seal	*Mirounga angustirostris*

Family OTARIIDAE: Fur Seals and Sea Lions

Sea lions

Northern or Steller's sea lion	*Eumetopias jubatus*
California sea lion	*Zalophus californianus*
Southern or South American sea lion	*Otaria byronia*
Australian sea lion	*Neophoca cinerea*
Hooker's or New Zealand sea lion	*Phocarctos hookeri*

Fur seals

Guadalupe fur seal	*Arctocephalus townsendi*
Galapagos fur seal	*Arctocephalus galapagoensis*
Juan Fernandez fur seal	*Arctocephalus philippii*
South American fur seal	*Arctocephalus australis*
Subantarctic fur seal	*Arctocephalus tropicalis*
Antarctic fur seal	*Arctocephalus gazella*
South African or cape fur seal	*Arctocephalus pusillus pusillus*
Australian fur seal	*Arctocephalus pusillus doriferus*
Northern or Alaska fur seal	*Callorhinus ursinus*

Family ODOBENIDAE: Walruses

Walrus	*Odobenus rosmarus*

Glossary

beachmaster: A mature male pinniped that has won control of an area of the rookery; he can mate with any females within that area.

blubber: A layer of fat beneath the skin of marine mammals like pinnipeds and whales that stores energy and insulates the body from the cold water.

DNA: Short for deoxyribonucleic acid, the chemical "blueprint of life" found in the chromosomes of the body's cells; DNA directs the cells to make the different life chemicals.

drift net: A fishing net that stretches for miles and can entangle air-breathing animals like seals and sea turtles and suffocate them.

eared seals: The scientific family Otariidae, sea lions and fur seals, which have a small external ear.

guard hairs: Long, coarse hairs in a mammal's coat that help support the finer, more abundant underfur.

harem: A group of females that lives in the territory of a beachmaster.

hemoglobin: A protein found in red blood cells that carries oxygen throughout the body.

kilogram: A measure of weight equal to 2.2 pounds.

krill: Small, shrimplike animals eaten by many seals and whales.

myoglobin: A protein similar to hemoglobin, myoglobin is found in muscles and stores oxygen. Animals like seals, that dive for long periods, have lots of myoglobin in their muscles.

PCBs: Short for polychlorinated biphenyls, toxic chemicals used in industry.

pinnipeds: A group of mammals which consists of all seals, sea lions, fur seals, and walruses; pinniped means "wing- or fin-footed."

pod: A group of pinniped pups that have been weaned and live together separate from the adults.

rookery: The breeding area on land of pinnipeds; also used for sea birds.

time-depth recorder: An instrument attached to a diving animal like a seal that measures how deeply the animal dives and the time taken by dives and between dives.

true seal: A member of the family Phocidae, which consists of pinnipeds with no visible external ear.

weaner: A seal pup that has been weaned.

Index